# A NECESSARY EXPLOSION

## COLLECTED POEMS

# ALSO BY DAN BURNS

Recalled to Life: A Novel

No Turning Back: Stories

A Fine Line: A Sebastian Drake Novel

Grace: Stories and a Novella

# A NECESSARY EXPLOSION

COLLECTED POEMS

# DAN BURNS

CHICAGO ARTS PRESS

ISBN: 978-1-7332794-3-7 (Hardcover)
ISBN: 978-1-7332794-4-4 (Trade Paperback)
ISBN: 978-1-7332794-5-1 (E-book)

Library of Congress Control Number: 2021900316

Cover art and illustrations by Daniele Serra
Book design by Salvatore Marchetti

Published and printed in the United States of America
by CHICAGO ARTS PRESS

Author Information:
www.danburnsauthor.com
www.facebook.com/danburnsauthor/
dan@danburnsauthor.com

10 9 8 7 6 5 4 3 2 1

First Edition

Dedicated to the memory of
my great aunt and first poetry mentor,
Anne Brunfleck.

# CONTENTS

# ILLUSTRATIONS

*Every morning I jump out of bed and step on a landmine.*
*The landmine is me. After the explosion, I spend the*
*rest of the day putting the pieces together.*

Ray Bradbury

*Afterimage*

# Afterimage

Memory is at best a shattered glass,
the shards strewn across the floor, and
I have not the time nor patience to
fit and glue all the pieces together.

I know it's there, the memory I seek, and
eventually it rears its head like an index card in
the catalog of an ancient library
that holds no books.

I see faces but no names, strangers, and
I tick, tick, tick through the alphabet,
hoping to trigger and cement
a neural connection that sometimes comes.

I used to worry that the lapses
might lead to the end of me, but
whatever the state of my mind,
my imagination will create, through my pen,

all I need to know and believe.
What is truly real anyway?
I close my eyes, calm my restless heart, and
the image, recalled, comes into focus:

I see hair the color of the dark chocolate paste
under the outer shell of a walnut, and
feel ghostly tingling in my fingers as
fine threads of silk pass through them.

A mask of porcelain,
tinted by a sun
south of the border,
near flawless.

Eyebrows that come
together as one when
left to their own devices
of natural progression.

A mouth so perfect
it need not speak
to tell me everything
that is in the heart.

And eyes that lead me
to a place of comfort,
pigmented with hues of the
mountainsides of Montana,

reflecting the meaningful
along with the meaning,
flashing a sparkle, a glint of
light from the big bang,

reminding me of everyone
I have ever loved, and
that image will remain
with me forever.

# The One

You—
are the only person you need to know,
a pupil dilated to enlightenment,
the prime reason for living,
an inspiration for every person
charmed by the sparkle of
hope in your eyes,
clearly clear about all the
people who have steered you
to this place in time and
the course they charted,
but understand it is
your turn to grasp the ship's wheel,
second to none,
destined to greatness to the
extent your humility allows,
one who can separate
fact from fiction and
truth from distraction
in a world of bobbleheads and charlatans,
poised to push the limits of possibilities,
able to live within and by
the boundaries of your life that
only you can define.

You—
are
the one.

# First Class

She first appeared as a blur, a ghost, in the collective peripheral vision of the travelers sitting in the first-class section of American Airlines flight 1329 to Chicago. Most did not know where she came from. Only the passengers in row six, the last row of the section, knew she was not from "their neck of the woods."

She walked up the aisle, slow and deliberate, with a single, uninhibited motivation.

Heads turned, eyebrows furrowed, minds raced. Before they could comprehend the invasion that had just occurred, she disappeared behind the closing door of *their* lavatory.

The businesswoman in 4D twitched with discomfort, her head turning back and forth, searching in desperation for the flight attendant.

The older gentleman in 2A, a retired neurosurgeon, scratched the inside of his leg as he sat ruminating on the laboratory experiment playing out in front of him.

A young woman in 5C, a breakout novelist on a nationwide book tour, smiled and returned to her book.

The section of the plane was eerily quiet, although the engines hummed and the wind outside seemed to roar. All eyes stared at the lavatory door. Time passed in slow motion.

The successful real estate investor from Los Angeles in 1B was holding his breath as he held in his pee.

The lavatory door opened and she stepped out. All eyes locked on her like a missile system. Without breaking stride, she cut through the aisle as though it were a fashion runway. Her hair flowed behind her and her complexion glowed.

As she passed each row, heads turned as if pulled by a gale-force wind. No one said a word. Eyeballs tracked her every step until she parted the dividing curtain, stepped through, and vanished into the land of the living.

1C turned to 1D but said nothing. 3C tried to remember the details of the blouse the girl was wearing. 1B thought about getting up to pee but remained seated. Then, as if synchronized, every person in the first-class section of flight 1329 breathed a sigh of relief and smiled, though a single thought lingered in each of their minds:

*I wonder if she will return.*

# On the Ledge

I.

An ancient creator of wondrous verse
climbs the worn, creaking stairs to
a windswept rooftop ledge,
seeking guidance from the heavens that
he realizes will never come.

He glances down with impaired sight
upon a heartless street of dreams,
unaware of anyone or anything
that might be lurking below,
for he is alone and on the edge.

He weighs a lifeless manuscript
in hands with fingers stiffened,
crippled and more like talons,
contemplating with growing despair
his last years of work and life.

The pages spill from his hands like
water flowing over a breached dam,
taking flight, fluttering on injured wings,
an airmail delivery to everyone and no one,
only a solitary hope remaining.

His final statement, the end of the story,
is a dispatch without meaning

for anyone but himself
to a distracted and oblivious world
that needs nothing from its elders.

He has nothing more to give,
the inkwell of creativity bone dry, and
he can no longer bleed to refill it,
but a searing realization of his coda
emerges from deep within his heart.

He crawls onto the ledge and straightens
as though acknowledging the great flag,
toes inching over the edge as
he sways in time with the wind,
ready to leave his final mark on the world.


**II.**


*Wait!*

He is startled and calmed
all in the same moment,
his body trembling, heart still,
wondering if what he heard was
the word of an angel or the devil.

He gathers his remaining strength to
maintain a stable rigidity on the ledge,
a momentary and welcome reprieve,
an ending of the ending,
from his planned Pollock-like exhibition.

*It's me, Lacey.*
He feels his heart flutter, a lost and distant sensation,
feels a gentle hand grasp his ankle then his wrist
with a radiating warmth that guides him down off the
ledge onto the solid footing of the tar-papered roof.

Her eyes are like diamonds in the moonlight,
a complexion of the finest porcelain,
full lips rouged the color of an apple, and
an expression that conveys a thousand sentiments
but settles on one: I care.

Guilt-ridden and heartbroken, he bares his soul,
recounts the recent murderous act, or was it suicide,
of the newest offspring to bear his name, and
the blatant and inconsiderate shaming
of Seshat, the Egyptian goddess of writing.

*Do not despair*, Lacey tells him,
as she places a hand on his heart,
*for the words will always be here, inside of you,*
*and all will be forgiven, as long as you*
*share your passion with the world.*

At less than half his age,
she possesses a depth of compassion
beyond her years and that of a thousand people,
along with a desire to comprehend the words
of a timeworn prophet of the human condition.

**III.**


He ponders this unexpected twist of fate,
the nearly extinguished ember in his chest
now growing into a raging flame of lust,
not for the flesh but the crafting of stories through
verse, the lifeblood that has nurtured his soul and
stoked his life for seventy-odd years.

*Tell me your stories, please, for*
*I need to know the mystery of your world.*
*Speak the images in your heart and mind, and*
*bring to light the secrets of the universe*
*buried in the depths of your soul,*
*vaulted within your protected borders.*

Such words, coming from a woman so young.
He had heard her speak before but never listened,
their prior passing glances and kind words
bouncing off the walls of the apartment hallway
never registered, could not penetrate
his hardened outer shell of artistry.

*All I have for you, Lacey, for anyone interested,*
*is a slice of a life lived, a chapter of collected breaths,*
*a friendly and engaging glance from Campbell's*
The Hero with a Thousand Faces.
*My face is old, wrinkled, and tired, but*
*it reflects all that I am and have been.*

*I did not think that anyone was interested*
*in the stories of a distant time and place,*
*told in verse from the perspective of a man*
*out of touch but still with something to say,*
*meaningful in any way I cannot say.*
*My only hope a single open ear and mind.*

*My poems are gone, dead, sprinkled on the street below—*
    *It does not matter—*
*Two years of my life wasted—*
    *Not wasted but lived and reimagined through your*
    *poems—*
*I have nothing left to give—*
    *Together, we'll rebuild every line, starting with the*
    *first.*

*In the beginning, we saw the coming of the end . . .*

## Silent Words

I believe
it is possible to
say something meaningful
when words are not actually
coming out of your mouth.

I search longingly, endlessly,
for those nonverbal cues that
come not from vocal cords
but instead the heart and
the deep well of the soul.

I'd rather hear a story
through action and movement,
where storytellers and their stories
are brought to life within
our grand orchestra halls,

through the friction of
a bow against strings and
the joyous reverberation
professing the purest form of
dedication, conviction, and love,

or see with my eyes and mind
the grainy, black-and-white films of old,
which stir my heart and give me pause as
I realize the insignificance of what
everyone in the world is talking about,

or gaze into the realm of
oil paint on canvas, where
words and the meaning of life are
conveyed through the megaphone that is
the artist's paintbrush,

or scan the faces of people I meet for
a raised eyebrow of intrigue,
the glint of sparkle in eyes of compassion,
lips more interested in a gentle kiss
than in fruitless sputtering,

or observe the human race as it should be,
one person holding the door open for another,
a dollar tossed into the can of a homeless person,
a kind wave and smile to a young child,
a warm embrace.

I consider the words on this page,
a reflection of one person's flash-moment in time,
where ink on paper makes a thoughtful statement
for consideration at another time,
for one, for many.

## Experienced Reason

A man and a woman sit at a sidewalk café
sharing stories of failed marriages and
asshole bosses and disrespectful teenagers,
searching, hoping for a connection or even
the slightest glimmer of similar interests.

The coffee drunk, the stories told,
their souls bared completely
beyond comfort or reason,
they sit quietly and think and gaze
into each other's eyes, wondering
if their paths might possibly cross again.

Time passes like a broken clock and
as his stomach growls and the sun begins to set,
he eventually loses hope, concedes, and sighs.
She looks down and sighs in response and
in tandem they stand and smile and
walk off in opposing directions,
thankful for the realization that
loneliness is not a reason.

## Coupled

Searing vision like firelight,
    burned into the irises and onto skin,
stops the heart, breathless, creating a passion not
    knowing where to begin.

A dazzling kaleidoscope of firing neurons,
    at once here, there, and everywhere,
powerful enough to propel the sails of imagination
    with more than air.

Fatigue replaced with energy of a thousand
    glowing suns from galaxies afar,
the past screams out, the future beckons,
    only one destination: the stars.

Morality, life, made clear, not through actions but
    words from the heart,
right snatched from wrong, and vice versa—
    can we tell them apart?

Fear of mortality vanishes as long as
    there are stories to share,
a mishmash of errant thoughts, then a message,
    always something to spare.

"All business" a necessary course of action to
    unearth the revelation due,
coupled with a steadfast demeanor, sometimes false,
    but still honest and true.

Skin like glass, everything exposed,
    the wall comes crashing down so fast,
like a posted placard for the world to
    see clearly at last.

## No Turning Back

Walk the road you come upon,
climb the mountain that rises before you, and
explore the wonder you see in your mind's eye.

No. Yes. Either response is an option, and a decision.

Tomorrow matters, and it is not yesterday.

Your path, your journey, and your adventure
are yours to make and take.

Go ahead and jump from the highest peak.

There's only one way to go and that is down, but
make it a thrill ride with a soft landing.

There is no time for rethinking past decisions or
living with regret, as what would be the point?

Always be thinking about "the next" aspects of your
life: the next book, love, day, experience, sight, sound,
taste, feeling, and memory.

History is in "the passed."

Walk forward and away, but glance back
every so often to let them see the fire in your eyes.

A goal is faith rooted in desire.

Sorry, but . . . forget it.

It is an art to put one foot in front of the other
while maintaining a full peripheral vision.

If you come to a fork in the road,
remember that your fork can have many tines, and
they are all going in the right direction.

Sometimes we hold on too long to the memories
that are, in fact, the anchors that drag us down.

Say "hello" and "welcome"
with a hearty handshake and hug, and
embrace what comes next.

Heaven is for wishes and hell is for regrets.

The last memory of you is replaced by the next one.

## Crazy Woman Creek

The roadside sign directed him to her.
He was a roaming, misguided, distant planet.
She was a lonely, dark star who
somehow pulled him into her orbit.

Crazy Woman Creek Rd – ½ mile.

He'd been traveling south on Interstate 90
through the vastness of northeast Wyoming,
his past tortured residency on the
road to rehabilitation a distant memory.

He was free.

He took the exit without thought and
weaved his way through the canyon,
effortlessly and seemingly on autopilot,
his awareness enraptured, enveloped by
the alternating rugged and majestic terrain
that calmed his restless heart.

In the distance, a rustic trading post
rose from the ground like an oasis,
its form a wavy apparition
baked by the sweltering heat.
A cowboy from another world
leaned back casually on the horse rail.

The cowboy told him about
the plight of Mary Morgan,
a once-gentle woman turned into
a tarnished and embittered soul.
Her husband and daughters
scalped by the Crow Indians, she was
left to endure the resulting madness.

Forever.

Legend had it that her spirit
loomed in the area, that she walked
the shores of the creek after dusk,
a tormented soul in limbo searching for
a transport to the other side.

With the last remnants of daylight remaining,
he found her creek around the next bend,
stepped into the rushing water, and
immediately felt her coldness and distance, but
he also sensed her longing for companionship.

With both feet in her waters,
he was grounded for the first time in years,
overwhelmed by her pain and longing for retribution.
Her waters flowed over his soul.

The wind whispered through the trees
as though speaking to him in
a language he seemed to understand,
even if not fully.

It was her.

Across the creek, he saw a
Crow warrior with full headdress,
face streaked with paint,
a bow slung over his shoulder, and
the warrior smiled and morphed into
a fifteen-point whitetail deer.

He heard the whistling of a songbird—
or was it the shriek of a crow?—
a moment before feeling the searing pain
of the arrow through his heart.
The sun returned, flashed before his eyes,
as the creek water splashed his face.

He thought he saw her in
the streaking brilliance of the
world below the waterline,
her auburn hair flowing through the rocks.
He heard the sweet lullaby of an angel
echoing in his ears.

He wondered if he was going insane . . .

Facedown in the cool, welcoming waters,
he felt all the innocence and compassion of life.
"My Mary," he said, through a water-choked gasp.
Their hearts and minds and bodies entwined,
they were one, a merging of spirits,
rising from the water, ascending
into the heavens, off on their
journey to the promised land.

He had questions that neither had
nor required any answers but
they quickly faded from memory.
She was the only answer he needed.
Unburdened, he took comfort in knowing
that she and he were
the sanest people of all.

*Worlds Traveler*

# Worlds Traveler

*For Ray Bradbury*

A young boy looked up into the night sky
searching the blackness for the meaning of it all,
longing for the call from the magical mistress
of all things sacred and noble
to set him upon the path to become
a storyteller for the ages.
He had a sense of wonder and a zest for life
not yet (and never to be) extinguished, and
he held his heart open to the gods
and waited.

She shot across the heavens,
a vision from the past and
an oracle of the future,
a fire-hot projectile
with enough fuel to propel her to the end of time,
and a long, glowing, and flowing tail
to light the way for all.

He gazed in amazement and
considered the spectacle.
What was it?
Who was it?
Did you see it?
Did you feel the warmth, the majesty?
He could not hear it, for it was silenced by distance,

but oh, did it make a sound.
He could not touch it, and yet,
it left an overpowering impression.
The boy watched and listened intently,
and took heart.
His decision was made.
He jumped on for the ride and never looked back.

Together as one they traveled into the future,
a celestial object made from the
dust of the stars and the love of the gods,
their measure and strength growing along the way,
fed by everything they touched.

He was instantly aged but ageless, timed but timeless.
His was an eccentric orbit on a determined course.
I could see the arc of his path clearly and
knew at once that the mystery and the magic,
the stories and the love, would never end.

The brilliant light traveled across the galaxy and
left in its path only love and insight and inspiration,
surely enough for mere mortals to build a life upon.
Surely enough for me.

I watched the blazing light streak across the sky
for as long as he would allow me.
I ached to follow his travels,
wished to garner some of the passion he held
for life and for words.

As I pass through what remains of
the radiant, cosmic particles left in his wake,

I take comfort in knowing that the pixie dust is
strewn far and wide, and I can only
hope that the light never dies.
I know that someday he will return, that
he will come back for all the world to see.
Maybe not within this lifetime, but sometime . . .

# Triptych

I think about life and death
and what lies in between.

I look left and right and
they are there beside me,
my brothers—we are
three, unmatched panels
held together by hinges
forged by the callused hands
of some higher being.

No matter how hard we try
to break free, the hinges hold.
We cannot break free—for
each of the three panels
contains its own pictures,
colors, brushstrokes, stories,
but they bleed over from
one panel to the next.

I can see my own image
but it is not yet finished,
will never be complete.
I need my brothers—
wings that allow me to fly,
for it,
the triptych,
tells the true story.

# The Fog Cutter

A communication came through
from a distant relation,
far and yet so near,
a memory held so dear,
inbound from another worldly plane,
with a message for the heart.

The words came through
like a cutter through a frozen sea,
clearing the fog away,
making the point to say,
*History is interpreted by*
*the open mind of the present.*

He wanted me to know
the clarity of his intentions,
not clouded by chemicals or the past,
or by characters for which he was cast,
that I should always know
he knew I was there, that we were there.

He sensed my recurring concern
regarding an unlikely genetic malady,
one that might rear its dastardly head,
to keep one living and at the same time dead,
in later years when the senses are fragile
and need no additional aggravation.

His sense was accurate indeed,
self-inflicted baggage carried for fifty years,
based on nothing but what I could see,
wondering only if it could happen to me,
but through our bonding during his final years,
we cleared away the always-present fog.

He knows that I know,
I know that he knows, and
no thought could be clearer,
even if he were nearer,
because absolutely nothing can
cloud the understanding of the heart.

# Black Crow

Another sleepless night,
harsh rain pounding against
my bedroom window, and
I'm left wondering if the
rumble in my stomach is from
the smoked salmon sandwich or
the crow I ate last night,
reliving decisions and actions
by themselves insignificant but
together enough to kindle
my restless heart,
to stir the cauldron of regret,
not for inaction but action,
for years feeling certain
I would only regret the
things I did not do but now
realizing not too late that
certainty is uncertain except
when it comes to living with
the past, the ghosts,
for all the days that remain.

# Daytime Dilemma

The dream fades,
a new dawn breaks,
the wind and rain and birds
knock at the window,
erasing the realm of
conjured, incredible insight,
urging an awakening,
a decision to flee or return,
wondering which side of
the razor's edge will
cut and bleed less.

The fight never endures,
waking inescapable until
the permanent dirt nap arrives,
initiating the endless dance
choking on dirt and darkness,
pushing up daisies;
alas, fear not, for
the new day arrives, like
the train of the vicious circle
that makes no stops on
the journey to enlightenment.

The inevitable, the day,
each moment in time a choice
between the devil and the deep blue sea,
one nipping at the soul,
the other at flailing heels;

but proceed undaunted,
swim through the calm straits of desire,
where the choices reside in the realm of creation,
all good and just.

The day, work or play,
variants of the same definition,
the latter a pursuit of loves,
purpose unrestrained,
never judged except by
the hand of the divine;
when presented with
two equally unpleasant choices,
dig deep, unearth a better third alternative,
the space between the rock and the hard place,
the sweet spot, swelling to overflowing
with true meaning.

At day's end,
the charted course
between Scylla and Charybdis
was no match for the righteous,
the plight of Odysseus averted,
the dawn decision well made, crafted,
securing the memories,
the fuel for the fire of
the next raging dream
looming on the horizon
that leads to tomorrow.

*A Song of Reason*

# A Song of Reason

I wonder what comes first,
the thought or the reason,
the melody or the words,
and realize I don't think it matters,
as long as they come.

The composition of music, of life,
is a miracle best cherished rather than
explained, or rationalized, or criticized.
But most of all, it must be nurtured.
The words and dots are the seeds to sow.
The instruments are the tools used to cultivate.
But the passion and the feelings and the love are
what send the words to the high heavens.

The artist feels the beat and beats the feeling.
She makes note of the notes and
sings the song, right or wrong,
and gets it all out before there is no more.
It's part inspiration, part perspiration, part reflection,
part projection, and all introspection.

The path is clear, yet not without
a thousand doors, heavy doors,
with many locks and many keys.
The soul is untarnished, and the keys
are there for the taking.

You can't get it out unless you're willing to go in.

# Concentric Circles

I stand on the bank of a quiet lake
in the early minutes of dawn
as the cool air pulls the mist up
from the heat of life below the waterline.

The stone in my hand is
a memory of yesterday, and
I throw it far in an act
of defiance and wonder.

The stone hits the water hard,
a bull's-eye with a splash, and
I hear the sound and wonder:
Did anyone else?

As the stone descends into oblivion,
a single ripple emerges and grows,
radiating out from its
center of power and will.

A dozen additional ripples emerge,
one after another and close behind,
pushing out to all
within their reach.

Starting strong,
ending weak,
like a day,
like a life.

The stone of memory, that day,
once graced with detail and color,
becomes faint and gray until
all that remains is calm.

I am cleansed,
free of the past now and
ready to take on the new day,
the experience that awaits me.

I look down the sedate shoreline,
left and right and down by my feet,
taking comfort in the sight of
a stone for tomorrow.

# Where Do I Go from Here?

I stand in the here and now, thinking that what I've accomplished is what it is and what will forever be. It's been a good run, performed to much applause and some criticism, but it's time to take a bow and move on, for the next production is in progress and there's more to do and show and see. There's more to live. I can't turn around, for fear of losing my way, and without my thinking about it, my leg moves and I step forward with conviction. Today is my springboard into tomorrow.

I STEP FORWARD, and I wonder: Is there a grand plan for me, or am I the planner? Am I an oracle with eyes wide open to search the unknown with wise interpretation, or am I a self-fulfilling prophet? Am I a dreamer, or an architect with a vision? Am I a wishful thinker, or an artful intellectual with a plan for how I might realize and experience my wishes? I can be all of these things, and I know that logic and reason and determination will guide me down a defined and more certain path.

I STEP FORWARD, and I think of the start of a new day, crisp and fresh from the light breeze brought up with the sun. I think of a new book, someone's story that waits for me on my desk. I think of a new relationship that looms around the next corner, and consider with curious anticipation any one of a million possible opportunities that might arise when I least expect it.

I STEP FORWARD, and I wonder what I would do if I could see into the future. Would I live life to help make my predestined existence a reality, or would I force the charting of a new course? I dismiss the thought as nonsense, for what's the point? I don't have the impending insight, and yet my options are the same.

I STEP FORWARD, and I realize that history has yet to be defined, and that it will be etched in stone, permanently inked in the pages of life's archive, and sprinkled across the digital universe only when the heart beats that one final time. But even then, history is not static. It continues to evolve through the perception and interpretation of anyone and everyone who cares. The truth is seen through many sets of eyes, some perpetually clouded, but most clear, insightful, and welcoming. The open heart of those special people who do care will need a starting point to embark on that historical journey, and I think about the point where I want them to begin. The last memory of me is replaced by the next one.

I STEP FORWARD, and I ask myself: What is out there, beyond our neighborhoods and our cities and our world, and does it matter, given that I'm just a speck in the grand scheme of it all? I think so. What is certain is that the hereafter is my time. The future is what I make it, and so I step in that direction. The steps may be small, one foot in front of the other, and yet they carry me forward with such strength and certainty.

I STEP FORWARD, for I have no other choice.

# Grace

Took out my key, saw two keyholes,
aimed for the one on the right.
Been five years and six months
since the last time I got drunk,
came home to bear her wrath,
only to live with it each day since.

I stood before her, wobbly and wondering.
She stood, prim and proper, a false demeanor,
sniffed me, made a face as though revolted.
Said she had been waiting all night,
scared and thinking I was dead,
but it was only seven o'clock.

She asked where I'd been.
Told her McNally had quit and I'd been promoted,
went out to celebrate, have a beer.
"A promotion? With a raise?"
I said, "I assume so," so
she called me an idiot.

"We're struggling as it is.
You understand how this works, right?
You work, you get paid.
You work harder, you get paid more.
Now, I'm going to see you less and get less.
I'm the loser in this one."

Yes, indeed, my brain said, and
I offered to take her to dinner, wondered how.
She sniffed me again, said, "You're drunk," and
"I don't want to go out—with you."
Now cut twice, only I didn't bleed but
my ears turned hot and red,
like an iron sword just pulled from the fire.

I fought back the urge, never felt before,
stepped closer and told her I loved her.
She leaned back, said, "I hate you."
I kissed her, she said, "I hate you."
I kissed her, and she kissed back.

The heat dropped from my ears,
merged with hers as we probed
with hands of ancient newlyweds.
My edge hardened and in the moment,
all I could think about were
her words: "You're an idiot."

My brain said, "Go!" but which way?
I had to stop, break free, for
I stared at a stranger.
Said, "Who are you?" and
she replied with the same question.

Exactly.

I took a deep breath, calmed,
eyes clear for the first time,
turned and cut my way through
the doorway without looking back.

# Spring Thicket

Admiring the new spring growth,
I stand before the thicket—
a stout and imposing presence
that spans the shoreline,
representing an awakening,
a recognition of revival and retaliation
against the savagery of winter.
The roots, trunks, limbs, branches, and leaves
from a mostly invasive lineage are welcome
since they hold the shoreline intact.
We all have our place and purpose.
This thicket stands as a fortification,
a gatekeeper to the other side,
where the fish swim in water
that endlessly calls for me.
Each spring the thicket grows taller,
reaching for the sun, moon, and stars,
searching and grasping for some heavenly guidance,
a home to a thousand birds just
up from the southern hemisphere to
take residence in our sleepy Midwestern hamlet,
home to a monument that stands like a
statue of Saint Francis with
branches like welcoming arms where
the birds can rest from their travels to
take in the cool and moist air and
battle with the fishes for
a million mayflies soon to hatch.
I should leave the thicket be, but

it blocks my selfish view, squelches
my need to see over and beyond.
I step inside to cut it back but
wonder about all that lives within.
Where will all the birds go?
I cut the thicket and it cuts back,
thorns lashing out like hypodermic needles
administering something sinister,
poking me to let me know
I'm alive and human to a fault,
scraping my flesh and drawing blood in defiance.
Our battle is short-lived and
I surrender my scythe to
Gaea, the mother of everything, for
I realize now that the thicket represents life,
like the beginning of time and the world, and
I am only a mere mortal, not meant to
pass through the thicket but
instead embrace and relish it.
So I walk as far as it takes me,
to a natural break
that leads me to the other side.

## Thoughts on a Summer Afternoon

Trees the colors of green found in
the 128-count Crayola box.

The lingering taste of roasted and moistened
coffee beans.

The changing direction of the wind.

Can I refrain from connecting
with the meaningless world?

Where will the next idea, the next word, come from?

A young woman with long, tanned legs that
extend from a short skirt.

Is it possible that the only poetry
I can truly understand is my own and
maybe that reality applies to everything about me?

A young couple at the next table, plotting a future.

Endless cars with no discernible
character or personality, but all with
an uncanny sense of mediocrity and sameness.

I wonder if I write for anyone but me, and
settle with myself that there is at least
one interested reader and that is enough.

The person who stumbled upon
the discovery of alcohol should be sainted
or knighted or at least recognized
in some grander light.

Is it really eavesdropping if the person talking
is forcing you to hear them?

Life is too short to spend time on
irrelevant and meaningless activities,
not the least of which is
a book that has not captured
your full interest and attention.

The innocence of a child.

I believe it possible to say something when
words are not actually coming out of your mouth.

Maybe I will shave my beard or grow it longer.

I like when there is room
in the waistband of my pants—
enough room to appropriately experience the day.

A glass of bourbon with a single ice cube.

You need to make a point to sit back and
take notice of what is going on around you.

But sometimes it is best not to listen to
the droning of those people who apparently
have nothing to look forward to.

There's something special about the feeling
of a pencil in your hand and the
scratching of lead against paper.

A good meal and a bottle of wine, followed by
a snifter of cognac and a cigarette.

The coming sunset and subsequent sunrise.

# Perspectives

A thousand people can read the same words,
each deriving a different meaning,
each correct in their own right and
as part of the composite.

Flipping a coin is a fifty-fifty proposition,
much like meeting a person for the first time,
which is why I now carry a two-headed quarter.

The winner of the argument is the one
with the decency and willingness
to understand the other person's perspective.

The difference between red and blue is
simply a variation in frequency and wavelength and
they are still both (beautiful) colors.

The line divides us, yet no matter what its height,
humanity dictates that we hop over and
stand side by side and see what they see.

A mirror's reflection is processed through
two imperfect and clouded eyes.

Whether vista or pigeonhole, the
depth of understanding is potentially similar.

A left turn is a right turn
for the person facing you.

Instead of taking a stand,
have a seat and crack open a book.

You may climb and I may descend and
the mountain is a big, sharp rock.

I filter what I see and hear through
the sands of my time;
take me for a walk on your beach.

Aim to see life from the third-person point of view.

What is ultimately under the covers but
a beating heart?

# Free

Boots crunch over stalks.
Irons in hand.
Father, leading son and pulling dog
into a clearing known for
life of another sort.

Skin pale and stretched,
covered with goose bumps.
Eyes dry but searching
for the slightest glint of feather
across the whitewashed backdrop of morning sky.

Father raises his iron and
shoots at the ghost of a bird.
The percussion reverberates musically, endlessly,
and we wait and hope
as our stomachs sing their own chorus.

A single bird emerges as if from nowhere,
a fluttering so sweet,
grace beyond imagination.
We track its path,
father and son and dog.
We track its path.

Father raises his iron once more,
leading the pheasant into the ether.
He stops, distracted.
We watch and listen
as the pheasant turns into a speck, diminished,
and we are left staring at
the blank palette of life.

# The Photograph

❧

The photograph, more than forty years old,
lies clean and flat like a monocle
reflecting the sands of time.
The white border is discolored,
yellowed from the fire of 1970 that permanently
stained the inanimate and animate alike.

The living room sits in a different time,
the furniture pieces like dinosaurs trapped in the
throes of a late-1950s art deco diorama,
a forgotten strain of decor only available from
the discount stores in town.
A color palette long-since buried,
put down and out of its (and our) misery
until the cycle comes full circle,
a birth in exchange for a death, and
I can only wish, hope, that it
never sees the light of day again.

On the wall are two birds, hand carved
out of some unnatural material,
lost and almost fluttering, and somehow
surprisingly present in an unusually large number of
family photographs over the years.
Where did the birds come from, and
what do they want?

*Ink*

# Ink

## I.

The front page of the newspaper
screamed at him in a fit of rage,
paused his beating heart.
He wondered how it was possible,
the senseless rants and acts of
people he thought were sensible.
He did not need to read the story,
for the headline and picture had
permeated his soul, were
fused into his memory.
He looked at his finger,
saw the ink there, and
wondered if he could
ever wash it clean.
It was the one tattoo imprinted
against his will.

## II.

"Sign on the line," the man urged.
*Why such a hurry?* he thought as
his hand reached for the pen
but stopped short.
He felt a bead of sweat trickle

down the middle of his back
that felt like a spider, poisonous, and
ready to give something while
taking something much more valuable
away from him.
"Sign it!" the man now demanded.
He could not.
He pushed back from the table,
wobbling to the door with fear, for
he knew the questionable implications.
It was the only tattoo
he could not accept.


**III.**


With an old but steady hand,
he scribbled feverishly,
the hourglass almost empty,
pouring the ink of his experiences
onto the pages of his life.
Most of the words were clear and precise but
others were horribly smeared
before they could dry with permanence.
His words, in his hand:
it was the only tattoo
he could live with.

## 'Bout as Nothing as You Can Get

My heart—
it's 'bout as nothing as you can get.
My love—
it would be best for you to forget.

The time we've shared this year,
some memories held so dear—
can there be more or less?
I fear less, I must confess.

Seems I'm gas to your fire,
anger overcomes desire.
Our time together can't last,
we're a volcano ready to blast.

It's time to make a change,
go—set off on the open range.
Leave now while there's time left,
fold now, place a new bet.

Love is a song played across the strings of the heart.
We're so out of tune, an orchestra torn apart.

My hope—
it's 'bout as nothing as you can get.
Your smile—
is the one thing I'll never forget.

If you stay, I'll never know
if our love will ever grow.
So take a walk and be free,
now the world is yours to see.

On your journey, I hope we'll find
if what we have was meant to bind.
While you're gone, I'll think of you
and strive to build my heart anew.

Never mind, I'm lost, come back and take a chance.
We'll start over with a lover's first dance.
If we're lucky, we'll build a love so true,
and forever, I'll give my all to you.

Love is a song played across the strings of the heart.
Let's compose our life together, never apart.

My doubt about us—
it's 'bout as nothing as you can get.

# Reflections

I waited an eternity of three-squared months,
and when you came, I missed you.
I thought I saw you, can see your image
clearly in my memory, but you were gone.
Nothing remains but a ghost in my imagination,
yet I see you, and I see me.

I look down into the rushing water
of my favorite river but it turns me away,
providing only a wavy apparition to consider.
Who is that and will he wait for me?
Will the face I see ever come into focus,
or is it meant to be blurred, mysterious,
and unrecognizable for eternity?

I push away the ghost of Narcissus
and try to find some meaning,
some loved one, or
possibly a past influence.

Everywhere I look, I am reminded.
A mirror or a pane of glass.
A passing glance,
an expression of acknowledgment.
A young face with even the slightest DNA match.

What we see is what we make of it:
reflection, projection, introspection, or
maybe just the perspective of a single mind's eye,
formulated by the dust of the cosmos and
comprehensible only to the individual.

# Fall Cleanup

The summer lies down for
a long-awaited and much-needed rest
while magically revealing to me
the empty stalks and limbs all around,
waving gingerly and desperately
like starving peasants.
The leaves are everywhere, colorful and dead,
waiting to be gathered up for one last farewell.

I remember.

The changing of the season propels me forward,
continuing the perpetual motion of life,
but it comes to me that the intervals are also
milestones of reflection in the serene pool of my soul.
I look at the leaves, and consider the leaving, and
I wonder about the exposure, and the truth.

There's nothing to hide.

To plant and nourish the seed and
nurture the growth until the time of harvest
brings me a relished culmination of progress.
Yet clearing away the dead brush,
I wonder if I'm paving the way for what is to come or
cultivating the memories and the history or
preparing for the future or
burying the past.

Is this the end or just the beginning?

The year past can be a time easily forgotten.
But there is an opportunity to recall
all that was once special and meaningful.
Down on my knees, as I pull the
dead vegetation from the dirt's gentle grip,
something from deep inside directs me to reminisce.
The earth, enriched with each season's cycle of life,
urges me to remember something long-since gone
that aches in me like a smoldering ember
that will never die out, that
I can only hope will blaze again.

The choice is mine.
I will remember,
I know this, and
yet I wonder:
Where do I go from here?

# Keepsake

He reached into the right front pocket, always the right front, of his Levi's. It was noon and for the fiftieth time, he reached in deep to make sure it was still there. It was and he felt it, cold and solid, with just a fingertip, and he knew he was going to be fine. The fiftieth time meant he could grab hold of it, grasp it tight, and extricate it from its cavernous vault. He looked down at his closed fist, his heart racing and pulse pounding behind the globes of his eyes, though he did not realize the sensations as his captive world plugged his ears with silence. The high sun was especially warm, but other forces manipulated his body temperature, the red zone quickly approaching. He tried to breathe easy, steady, and after exactly fifteen counted breaths of the stale air around him, synapses fired, a key turned, and as an unwitting accomplice, he sent the message. His fingers relaxed ever so slightly and opened slowly, methodically, like the doors of a missile silo. His fist became a platter, holding the precious archaeological find ever so gently. He bowed his head, cautious but reverent, to observe it more faithfully as a droplet of moisture fell from the tip of his nose and landed on the long, burnished nail that rested in the palm of his hand.

# Liar, Liar

I can live my life as
though it weren't mine,
forget about passion and
leave conviction behind.

I can pretend government
will never drop the ball,
and sit back while
talking heads question it all.

Seeing someone in need,
I can just stroll by,
walk past a burning building
with eyes to the sky.

When dreams slip away,
I can simply not care,
and the regret leaves me
with nothing to bear.

I can say all these things and
let life pass me by,
but to know me is to know
that it's all a big lie.

# Distant Memories

A passing of pure love,
the first blink of light,
the alien taste of copper,
a saintly maiden aunt with a writer's DNA,
the sneering but playful eyes of
a brother looking down from the bunk above,
a regurgitated breakfast (with peas?)
displayed on the school playground
on the first day of kindergarten,
the sickening crunch of dog bone under
the wheel of a bicycle,
the first gut-wrenching death,
two warm-blooded anchors
holding firm in a tumultuous sea,
the move from flat asphalt to shingled roof,
a blazing fire that chills to the bone,
a grandmother's endless inspiration,
the ghostly recollection of a little brother
who had somewhere else to go,
a love for the game,
a pseudo-illusionist's unfortunate misdirection
and a self-directed and forceful revenge,
images of film burned into the gray matter
until the end of time,
the inability to let go,
the gentle but significant transformation
from lemming to lion,
words that quicken the heart,

a tearful goodbye
and a heartfelt hello,
the fear of the unknown,
the foundation of life and love, and
the instillation of the pure essence of
all that is right in the world.

# Totem

I may not carry them but
the words are always with me.

Once a book is part of the family,
I can never disown it—
I will cherish it forever.

Sometimes my books travel with me, but
often, they gather amongst themselves,
sharing and collecting their own stories while
waiting, partaking, and bonding.

The book defines me,
represents what I am and
what I aspire to become.
The book is my teacher, mentor, friend,
inspiring and influencing me and
steering me down paths
familiar, foreign, interesting, and adventurous.

The book is a vehicle for
passing on the necessities,
the meaning of life;
for me to pass along to others.
The book is me.

# Hello, Again

We haven't talked in so long that
the vision of your face has blurred and
your smile has faded and
I long to see them both clearly again.

The words come with strain,
in fits and starts,
with intermittent clarity.
I hope that through all that
is vague and unclear
there is some structure,
some meaning to discover.

I want you to know all there is
to know since you went away,
since the day you departed
on your endless journey to the other side.

I need you to know.

I never cared about approval or consent
for what was always meant to be.
But as the years disappear there
grows in me a journeyman of a different sort,
one who blazes a trail
but who for some odd reason
needs confirmation that the
path is clear and meaningful.

I need to know.

The letter I wrote to you
is everything that I am now and
likely all that I will ever become.
Smile for me once again,
bring it all into focus one more time
and set me on a guided course where
I can see you at every turn.

Leave with me your bright and shining light.

# Twitch

I remember the little jerk, the twitch that
the mind triggers, firing neurons,
just before I fall asleep.
It happened last night and I'm glad it did.
The twitch saved me.

More often than not,
I lie down at the end of the day and
fall into a deep sleep like a mummy:
stiff, oblivious, and uncaring.
But not last night.
Last night was different.
Last night was memorable.

I was more tired than usual,
had been on my feet for more than fifteen hours,
energized only by coffee and vodka.
I started with coffee, ended on vodka,
aware of the obvious, incorrect order.
The vodka usually suppresses the twitch,
but like I said, not last night.

My head hit the pillow, my mind elsewhere.
The dream might have started earlier.
I can't say how long it took, but
the twitch came and it hit hard.
It woke me with a jolt and I
kicked the footboard with all my
uncontrolled and unconscious might.

Semiconscious but alerted,
I thought about the pain in my big toe,
hot and searing pain, but it left me quickly.
The pain was replaced with fear and
heart-stopping dread.
He was standing there at the foot of the bed,
pointing a gun directly at my head.

*The Book Thief*

# The Book Thief

There are too many books for the time remaining,
for within the pages lurk meaningful insights
from people who matter, their stories
based upon careful thought, consideration, and
endless revision, not thoughtless
sound bites but thoughtful reflections.

There are too many words and stories
for the time remaining,
the published book the only tangible legacy left
for one whose single purpose is to empty
a mind filled with stories that the world
needs to know and understand.

Distraction waits in the periphery,
in the shadows and around every corner,
like a drug dealer expecting a visit from a junkie
needing a fix, looking over shoulders and
eavesdropping to secure the moment and
then it happens, often unbeknownst to the victim.

His form is flexible and ever changing,
a distant and out-of-touch contact dispensing
not the targeted strike of a single,
troubled soul but everyone's,
presented as an overlay of sights and
a bombardment of stimulation,

sadly, not of world events or any
issue of importance to man but
instead, an endless drivel of
blah, blah, blah.
The moments stolen, one after the other,
are time I cannot afford to lose.

The diversion, standing tall like the Great Wall
between my books and me and the world,
drives me into a frenzy,
a maddening unhinging, and
I must break through for
my limbs cannot handle the climb.

My concentration is in
the hands of a technological puppet master,
but I own and wield
the scissors necessary to
cut the strings and
be free.

# Home Away

We travel to get away, to break free from the daily grind and re-energize the mind, the body, the life.

We travel to leave behind the endless activities that fill our days, so we may instead fill each waking moment with something potentially more meaningful.

We travel to discover, explore, and learn about other people and their cultures and mysteries. Most of all, we travel for the journey and the resulting experiences, for experience is the thread that makes up the fabric of our lives.

We embarked on a journey to lands unknown, lands that would very soon become familiar. In due time, Spain shared many things with us. I will forever be reminded of great museums and the ghosts they accommodate, the inspired art, waving flags, wine, olives, the World Cup, history, brilliant architecture, culture, tapas, music, cathedrals, street musicians, paella, and the Black Madonna. Spain was all of these things, but it was so much more.

For a two-week eternity, Spain was our home, and a home is what you make it. Each of us brought special things along to remind us of where we came from, and we brought our knowledge, our plans, and our expectations to help shape where we were going. We brought our dreams. We brought each other.

Spain welcomed us warmly into its cities and shorelines. Our family brought the rest. No matter where we go, as long as we have our family, then we have a home.

Looking back, I realize that I had never before, nor have I ever since, felt so alive, so energized, and so darn good in all my life, and that is a memory I will carry with me forever. I hope someday to have the opportunity to experience Spain again, for it has so much more to offer, and deep down I feel my journey with Spain has only just begun.

Until next time.

# After the Rain

Sponge-soaked clouds
squeeze their final drops
upon a world stained
by time and life.

Whatever the water touches
is cleansed without knowing why,
by whom or how an even
more remote possibility.

The clouds recede
into the distance,
absorbing and dropping
over and over again,
a cycle perpetuated
across the globe,
dictated by God.

The sun looms on the horizon,
rays passing through every
falling droplet, a host to
different wavelengths
bent to form and reveal
all the colors represented
in the rainbow of life.

# The Fog

## I.

Under an influence of force
more sinister than money—namely, power—
he rallies the masses in retaliation.
After reviewing footage from
a kaleidoscope camera and
pages of legislation so dense,
as if written with invisible ink,
he signs the order with a ceremonial pen,
the nib leaking blood, and
with a robotic wave, declares war.

## II.

A laminated world map unfurled,
splayed open like a dead fish.
Opposing forces line up
thoughtfully and with precision
like small, plastic, play soldiers
praying for a windless day.
Each side stands at the edge, steely eyes
wishing the other into submission and
they tense, first hearing and then feeling the
coldness of a stern wind picking up.
They watch in horror as a single

soldier topples forward.
Then all hell breaks loose.


## III.


With eyes wide open and stunned,
they watch the storm roll in.
On ground and in the air, it is
a force of nature, yet unnatural.
They watch the erupting, smoking guns
amidst the mist of tropical waves, wondering:
Is it a cloud of infinite cigarettes or
something more, like the
pungent smoldering of a burned village?
They put up a transparent barrier to forget
the pain, fear, and wrongness of it all,
for they never want to know or remember.


## IV.


We listen and watch with clipped heartbeats,
raising flags and pledging allegiance
while slinging irons and planning in haste for
the haunting, if only slightly probable,
end of the world and our civilization as we know it.
As days pass, bombed more by media
than apparently harmless exploding ordinance,
routine and mundane life events and propaganda

cloud our minds unwittingly,
consume us, and take us as prisoners.
We put up a transparent barrier to forget
the pain, fear, and wrongness of it all,
for we never want to know or remember.

*And even if we do want to remember, we forget.*


## V.


At their school desks,
minds open to endless possibilities,
books cracked open to the words and
images of a distant time, a forgotten horror,
they struggle with the stories,
the meaning and reason,
the decisions of named and nameless faces
wearing rose-colored glasses.
They struggle, for their innocence is clear,
not clouded by anything but purity and happiness,
unimpaired by the vivid images from the
flesh-and-blood memory recorders of their ancestors.
Our only hope is that the real stories
make their way into the fabric of the children
so they may lead us down
a path of friendship and peace.

# In Motion (or So It Goes)

So it goes, day after day, the perpetual activity that passes the hours, and I often wonder what the point is, unless I can grab hold of something real, an event or accomplishment, that I can etch not just into memory, but also into a wishful archive of history, so I make the daily journey to the office and place myself before the Muses, with a solemn and steadfast reverence, and I wait and spur on the creation of a story I know is there, awakening the unconscious treasures to mesh with the real and the imagination of a mere mortal with half a century of planted seeds that have grown into something but I don't know what, and I take comfort in knowing that IT is there, but an idea left unwritten is simply an unfulfilled dream, for it will dissipate into the ether with no more applause than for the passing of wind, so I sit before my machine and eventually my fingers move and I dare not stop until I have bled onto the page, one word or ten or a thousand, it does not matter, because with each word the idea, the life lived, becomes real and the satisfaction that accompanies accomplishment becomes real, awarding me the earned right to live another day as a writer, because I have indeed written, something, that I can touch and feel again and mold into something finer that might someday touch someone else, that being the real point, to leave an impactful mark on another person, of this generation or the next or the next one after that, and if I can make that connection through my writing then I am content, for now, but when I leave my cage there is more I must do to continue to leave my imprint on the fabric of life, first and foremost with those special people I hold dear, my family, but then on to each person I may meet, and the goal is to arouse a smile, the universal sign and expression that all is right in the world, give and receive, and if I cannot write nor smile and be smiled at then I have no other option than to grab my fly rod and walk the banks of my favorite rivers in search of a more basic connection with the natural world, feeling the flow of rushing waters against my legs as I long to find the riffle or settling pool that holds hidden creatures camouflaged from the world above yet sometimes visible as a streak of lightning, and if my stealth approach and patience and mediocre skill are worthy, then I might be so lucky as to witness the strike and gentle fight of a majestic fish that reveals all the colors of the rainbow, and with all of this, these daily goals and experiences and revelations, I can celebrate a life well-lived, for one more day, and so it goes . . .

# Composition

The new day awaits,
a clean canvas,
a fresh palette of colors,
an unwrapped brush,
waiting for the hand of inspiration to
transform the forthcoming experiences—
lines, curves, and splashes of emotion—
into an impression of a moment in history.

The pen and journal await,
masked in a shroud of looming clouds,
only the flowing ink able to reveal the light,
the words linking together fragments
by themselves insignificant but together
the only genuine revelation of the truth,
exposing the hidden mysteries of the mind
in the only form that matters, the story, that
someone who cares can interpret and understand.

A song of inspiration awaits,
a lifetime of notes and lyrics read,
harmonious sounds heard,
the often-fragile heart shocked,
leaving only the steadfast determination
to press fingers on strings and strum or pick
repetitiously and relentlessly until
the skill develops, builds, and forms into
the ultimate expression of love,
inspired music from one heart to the next.

The end awaits in the shadows,
today, tomorrow, or years from now,
one can never know for certain,
so every moment must somehow be
etched into the annals of history,
every pixel of experience critical to
the unique composition of an image,
an impression, that will last forever.

# Gratitude

An unfamiliar face approaches
from an unknown place
wishing only to share
a thought,
a feeling,
a tug of the heart,
all driven by the mere stringing of
one word after another
by the figment of a person
chasing a dream.

Listening intently to
the thought,
the feeling,
the tug of the heart,
I clearly realize the true
magic of story,
for if you were to ask
a thousand faces you would easily get
a thousand different perspectives and
all of them are good and meaningful,
so much so that whether the perspective
is harsh or glowing,
what is important is that
the effort was made and
the effort alone must be
cherished and
honored and
embraced.

# Immortal Sin

How strange it must be, must feel,
to be gone and yet still carrying on
like dust in the wind that somehow circles back,
casting a much wider net.

Remembrance.

Imagine that there can be nothing worse than
darkness coming too soon in the autumn sky,
summer dreams unfulfilled,
and the unrequited hope for just one more day.

Longing.

It's bad enough to carry the unfulfilled
through to the end of days, but then, to
carry it beyond the hemispheres and
into the netherworld must be worse than hell.

Regret.

Take a breath and savor the spices of life and
know that each one will taste different until
such time as you have relished them all, leaving you
with the greatest story you could ever tell.

# Madness

Fingertips upon reality,
grasping for the slightest hold,
lingering traces of what I see,
the truth is never told.

Fabric strands of sanity
pull at both ends of thought,
images not what they appear to be,
fear them or be caught.

A gene pool of instability,
traces of evil and good,
tugging me toward a destiny,
uprooted me from where I stood.

Set adrift to explore what is "me,"
lost in a turbulent sea,
an anchor reaching for an extremity,
all I want is to be free.

Is it all slipping away?

*A Necessary Explosion*

# A Necessary Explosion

Cranial pressure can be defined as
the subjective measurement of
the worrisome crap accumulated
within the confines of one's skull
that directly impacts the quality of life.

Each day concludes with
impressions left by the world—
love, hate, commendation, criticism,
humility, ego, and opinions of
people who have imprinted themselves upon us—
and we're left to decide if
the words and their meanings
come from friend or foe,
are meant for support or destruction.

The pressure, contained by a God-made shell
intended to gather all the goodness of humankind,
builds and dissipates eventually, as designed,
as it must to ensure survival,
but the outcome can go either way.

We need more space for the meaningful:
knowledge, words, ideas, desires, humor,
history, stories, feelings, poetics, life, creativity,
love, talent, lust, skill, and music.

Fortunately, everyone has a release valve,
a "purge-erator" of self-preservation,
to disperse into the depths of the netherworld
everything meaningless and toxic.

Flush.
Cleanse.
Take out the trash.
Make the decision.

The tiniest shred of an idea is
a story waiting to be unleashed,
although it struggles to climb to
the top of the garbage pile in one's head,
to harness the heat of the morning sun and
light the wick, a strand of fibrous material
coated with a thousand life incidents
waiting to be ignited, each to burn as
part of the previous one and the next,
on the way to the ultimate climax.

Light the wick and get rid of it all,
blow up the trash heap and start fresh,
and let all the good of the world flow
from thought to pen to paper
for as long as the hands of time allow.

Only by releasing the accumulated energy
is one left with the golden flakes,
to analyze and forge together
and begin anew, even if not completely.

# On the Brink of Discovery

Two sheep stand at the edge of the precipice,
a lush green pasture under their cloven hooves,
blue skies off into infinity, but
over the edge and down below lurks
a blackness broken only by a
million blinking stars and a lonely moon
lit by an unknown source.

The sheep seem to know that
to step over the broken, rocky ledge
will mean certain death, but
they are torn, for they are
creatures of instinct, followers, and
there is no one left to follow but each other.
They look around, curiously, and wonder
where the shepherd and the
rest of the flock have gone.

The precipice represents the great divide
between reality and dreams,
between logic and facts and
the irrational delusions of a madman, and
the sheep struggle to make sense of
their perceptions, but they *can* assess,
for they are smarter than they think, or we know, and
they pause and contemplate:

The fine thread between day and night.

The heart-flutter of hope and despair.

The inherent comedy of their daily lives.

Were the earliest Greek philosophers insane and
was Columbus's course misdirected?

Is there a god, and if so, why has she waited so long
to lead us to this new, promised land?

Shall we remain in the pasture of comfort or leap
into the adventure of the unknown?

The sheep rest in the tall grasses and graze.
Distraught that their brethren have left them,
they take comfort in knowing that
they at least have each other and can wait,
together, for as long as they wish,
until the answer arrives.

## Already There

Visions of grandeur
define a strict bearing toward a place I need
to visit,
to explore,
to conquer.

Endless days and nights
overwhelmed with only
one line of thought and action,
one goal,
one promise.

At the crossroads, I forge ahead
to grasp the prize.
I hope it's what I expected, but
I wish,
I wonder.

Sitting streamside with recollection
of a history blurred by distraction, I can only sense
the rushing water,
the waving wheat,
the flight of a bird.

The sights, sounds, and scents
of the natural world calm
my restless heart,
my mind,
my soul.

And I realize I'm already there.

# Sculpture

A blank page
like a block of stone.
Nothing is there
but it is all there.
The treasure buried deep,
waiting to be unearthed
by the chisel of a craftsman.
Anguish builds like a volcano
on the brink of eruption.
Eventually the words come,
fingers pounding keys,
imprinting memories.
Ancient experiences reimagined as
a new tale for a future generation.
The blankness of the square form,
emblazoned with a new vision.
Imagination chipping away
the layers of fear and apprehension,
all that should not remain,
leaving only
the blood,
the story,
the truth.

# Blue Blanket

When I last saw it, the shape of it made me think that my mother had just emptied the lint trap of the dryer and left the furry mess on top of the counter in the basement. My older brother was staring at it, distraught and crying. He was five years old and attending his first funeral.

The fur had once been his blanket, blue and soft with the scent of summer air and loyal until the end. It had been his closest member of the family and now it was gone. Emaciated and withered, the blanket had nothing left to give. Only its skeleton remained.

Ever since the day he figured out his opposable thumbs, he'd lovingly picked at the blanket, pulling its love and leaving an endless stream of fibers in his wake, wherever his travels led him. The blanket gave, and gave, and gave until only a memory of it remained.

# A Landscape Changed by Time

Camp Wolverine South lurked like
a ghost, as a spirit in limbo,
wondering and waiting and hoping for
the call back to the big leagues.

The pool, once filled with
an ocean of cool wetness and waving limbs,
now filled from the sands of
a thousand encroaching tides, and
I wonder why the job is half done.

The still-blue (but faded and cracked) pool edge
stares at me in desperation,
half buried and longing to rise again as
the camp did so many years earlier.

The thirty-foot radio tower
looms over the land,
signals transmitting but with
nothing on the return leg.

It's out of place, like
a skyscraper in the Himalayas, and
it's polluting an area
historically unspoiled by
the trappings and distractions of technology.

Where do the lost memories go?
Did the caretaker toss them away
with the other rubbish or
is he waiting for a sign or
a signal (or a raise?) so he can
release them back into
the consciousness of life?

I recall an ancient lyric,
now out of favor but
at one time innocently sung by
young boys at the closing campfire:
*I wish I was in the land of cotton,*
*old times there are not forgotten,*
*look away, look away, look away, Dixieland.*

# Walking Through the Fire

A field of blazing coals so hot,
wind from the north and east leading to
cool grass and welcoming foothills beyond,
time is fleeting, you have only one shot.

Stoke the fire or wait for the rain,
each is a choice, but for those truly alive, with
blood raging through hardened veins,
take the first step, fear not the pain.

Better to harden the edge of your soul
with a fire fed by your words and faith and desire,
for Neruda said, "Theirs is blind wisdom," and
only your pen and story can make you whole.

Choose carefully the stones on which you step,
for some will singe, others will burn, and
still others will provide a cool respite
to ignite your heart, keep you nimble and adept.

Forge ahead with purpose, mindful and strong,
feel and embrace the fires of every burning moment,
every flash of searing inspiration, and
harness the heat to propel you along.

Eventually, the fire will fade and stall,
the sun will set one final time behind
the cold granite face of the jagged mountain peak,
leaving a history of undying memories for all.

# The Simple Truth

Fact or fiction?
Who the hell cares
except for what
actually puts the
heart in check and
bread on the table.

Deep down we're all alike,
from different places but
still the same world,
walking upright with
brains in the cranium so
what's the real argument?

We're all going to live,
we're all going to die, and
all that matters is what happens
in between those bookends,
the resulting marks left
on the history of humanity.

We all shit the same
and it all stinks, and
to think otherwise is a fallacy,
a delusion that must dissipate
if we seek any hope
of sustaining the human race.

We're all heading down the same path,
the only difference being
the road taken, and
all roads lead to
a terminating junction where
the train of redemption awaits.

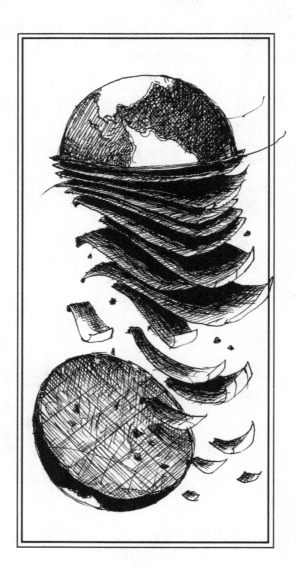

*In the Midst of a Revelation*

# In the Midst of a Revelation

I am in the midst of a revelation regarding the coming end of the world, which is inevitable, given the roiling state of the global financial markets, where greed is the sole driving force but for which there is no pot of gold at the end of the rainbow, and instead there is only a deus ex machina, a "god from the machine," a contrived plot resolution where there is only one possible outcome, that being a mass destruction and extinction of the tulip fields, the resulting barren land worth nothing, the landowners and farmers and buyers of the slender and alluring beauties holding nothing but dead remnants of dreams while the few lucky speculators hold the apparent keys to the world, feeling like gods themselves, and for what end but the amassing of an unearned fortune and an overinflated windbag of self-praise for what is nothing more than the lazy and ill-inspired will to trade a soul for a one-night stand with Lady Luck, and that love for her will surely die a severe and sudden death (for she loves no one) when the amassed wealth has no buying power in a world where the defeated and downtrodden and angered peoples resort to their animal instincts, all that remains perfectly intact when all sense of human nature is stripped away and the old game of "survival of the fittest" is in play, where the sides quickly form based upon global positioning, religion, class, culture, and, of course, race, but not government, for all the ruling parties across the globe will crumble down upon the fissured foundations that initiated the mania in the first place, and they will run and hide and let the hand-to-hand combat ensue until there is nothing left, not even a single hidden dream, like the hope of obtaining something for nothing that initially set the wheels of delusion and destruction in motion . . . triggering the beginning . . . of the end.

ATTENTION. THIS IS A MESSAGE FROM THE EMERGENCY ALERT SYSTEM. THIS IS NOT A TEST. WE REPEAT, THIS IS NOT A TEST.

# Requiem

A hallowed hall
hushed with anticipation,
welcoming the past
through a vision of the present.

An assemblage of strangers
bound by invisible chords
in search of meaning, the truth,
conveyed in an ancient script.

A composition of genius,
unfinished but still whole,
corners rounded by charlatans
seeking the master's unwanted treasures.

A reverent interpretation
by the heart of the world,
sounds pouring forth like gospel
from the flesh and the inanimate as one.

Remembrances of a bygone era
catapulted into the future,
a night of Munich music,
a mark in history, a memory forever.

Hearts pause,
imprinted with wonder.
Minds wander,
stretching boundaries.

Outsiders searching
inward then beyond,
the realm of possibility
there for the taking.

Now just within reach,
an outstretched hand
hoping to grasp
a sliver of humanity.

# Hope

Mrs. Magill watched with sadness
as the last child exited her school bus.

A month ago, she buried her husband.
A week ago, the school cut her pay.
Yesterday, she was robbed.
Today, she will give her notice.

The child turned and smiled.
"Thank you. See you tomorrow?"

Indecision.
Smile.
Hope.
Decision.

"Yes."

# The Paris, France, Suite

## I.

Paris by foot is
the only way to
see, hear, and smell
the birth of the day
on a Sunday morn.

In fact, having no map
guides the adventurer
searching for realization,
hoping for a detour,
embracing whatever may come.

Sometimes the best experience
is the one not planned but
stumbled upon.
I long to stumble
for all my remaining days.

## II.

Musical inspiration on the Rue de Rome,
a carved cello rising from a stump,
a Grafton saxophone from 1950 alive and well,
the opera hall filled with ghosts,

singing concrete gargoyles flying above,
stained glass like a mosaic rainbow
depicting *The Creation of Adam* and
all that has mattered since,
looking up for inspiration then
finding all I need for sustenance before me.

The evening quiet,
a day of memories fulfilled,
I am left thinking about
the misdirected souls
walking the echoing streets,
unable to see the light
of the coming day.

## III.

Art is art—
leave it at that.

Through the artist's craft,
he is able to materialize
all the mysteries of the soul,
is able to wrestle his demons to
flush out some sense of
the neuroses and fragmented realities
welled up in his heart and mind.

The product of craft, the art,
is the final statement,
all that needs to be said.

Then, the interpretation is in
the mind of the beholder.
Nothing more is required or
necessary from the artist.

Art is art.
Leave it be and
shut the hell up.


## IV.


I walked up a mountainside in Paris
to meet a man from Catalonia,
stumbled through the streets of Montmartre,
distracted by the sights and smells of
meats, cheeses, and wines,
all I might ever need for sustenance,
yet I remained steadfast,
hoping for some grander spiritual enlightenment.

At the top of the hill, distracted again
by the Sacré-Coeur Basilica,
I was touched by the grandeur,
inspired by the architecture,
wearied by the circular staircase to the heavens,
but as I left the cathedral and
descended the ivory steps,
I realized my guide was at a different cathedral.

Venturing through winding streets,
a different sanctuary emerged,

stairs descending into a world of make-believe,
a room opening up to the creations of another god,
a master of realization not quite real but
it seemed I understood his message clearly,
his unrelenting honesty of craft
bringing beauty to the world through sculpture,
paintings, and drawings from the heart.

The man spoke to me through his muses.
One, a woman on a crutch who
opened her world to me through
the drawers of her slender body, and
I looked and wondered while
clocks melted all around,
stopping and securing the moment,
telling me everything I needed to know
about fearless and unbridled expression.

He was there in the cavern, the man I sought,
rolling in a flickering display of
light through an acetate conveyor belt,
his words foreign but somehow intelligible,
asking me to understand but not judge,
for his bare soul was on display.
He hoped I might accept him,
his art and craft fueled by
the blood and sweat of his experience.

Leaving the sanctuary, I felt
the burning desire to genuflect, for
I was in the presence of a higher being,
a man who spoke the truth via
every imaginable physical medium,

his caring but tired eyes sparkled
while his curled and upturned moustache
said goodbye almost in defiance,
but I could not say goodbye—
hello was more fitting.


**V.**


Navigating through what may be
the largest concentration of
the greatest works of art in the world,
I was struck between the eyes
by the searing, unbelievable dichotomy
between art and art appreciation,
the latter a relative and variable term.

*Mona Lisa* and *Venus de Milo*,
their creators da Vinci and Alexandros,
watched in wonder at the gathering crowds,
every person blind but with a camera eye
that might somehow see and
record the true meaning of art,
an improbable wish.

An old train station,
locomotives replaced with
paintings and sculpture,
furniture and clocks like the face of the moon,
coexisting with a quieter, calmer
set of eyes and hearts
in search of the slightly more obscure.

Quieter and calmer still,
walking through what felt like
the Garden of Eden on Earth,
I befriended a man, sitting and thinking,
and I sat and thought with him.
As though with a good friend,
no words were necessary.

Even as I approached the *Gates of Hell,*
I was not fearful, for how could I be,
when the bronze doorway contained within it
the passion of thirty-seven years and
the meaning of life since the creation of man.

What better way to end the day than by
sitting at the shoreline of the water lilies,
straining to hear the birds sing, the frogs croak,
but I only heard my heart beating.
As I headed home to my quiet quarters,
I was fortunate to meet a man
whose vision was distorted but
I saw what he saw quite clearly,
could feel in my chest, my heart,
his struggle for balance
between reason and madness,
because I have walked in his shoes.

# The Nice, France, Suite

## I.

Requisite planning and preparation time condensed,
waiting time until departure lengthened,
necessary cabin pressure imprecise,
essential liquid and solid nutrients elusive,
Devil's request for bodily discomfort granted,
attainment of benefits from REM sleep denied.

I'm left somewhat jilted with
a vision that will not focus,
a subtle pin-like stabbing behind my eyelids,
a brain that feels like scrambled eggs, and
the sleep schedule and delusions
of a man walking a fine line
between reality and dreams.

Thank God for tomorrow.

## II.

My legs have paced a hundred miles
but there is no pain or fatigue.

My parched lips need only
the bold and fruity reds of Bandol.

Hunger comes often but does not last,
although the French sardine dish of my dreams
eludes me . . .

For now . . .


## III.


Art is art.

The artist thinks, prepares, envisions,
sees the end result clearly, and
with his tools unearths the
vision of his experience and subconscious,
hidden but found at last.

I may not "see" the art he created,
likely because I am not
looking through his glasses,
but it is there, and I owe it to him to
search for the meaning.


## IV.


From the outside looking in,
like a giant poking his toy globe:
a miniature port of matchstick boats;
gold-plated thimbles nestled on the mountainside;

111

azure waters of the gods
carrying the winds of the Mediterranean,
salted and refreshing for
the mouths of the thirsty.


## V.


The church's heavy door slammed closed,
sealed tight, not fearful but
submissive to what may be
the final heated judgment of us all,
no way out but with the key of music.

Where does a musician's true heart come from
when presented with the apparently insurmountable
task of performing in the realm of the unimaginable?

It can only come from God—
whatever or whomever that may be.

Each performance presented in front of a
loving and appreciative firing line,
her blindfold removed, she must
coax the love from her strings
while bound in a skin of armor.

When her comrades fall,
no one flinches but heartbeats quicken,
she can only pick them up and
carry them home.

Who's the god?


## VI.


Up, up, ever higher,
traveling upon a snake road that
often turns back on itself
before reaching again
for the sky and the villages
living just beneath.

One final switchback, and
I'm at the top of the world,
seemingly standing upon the clouds,
expecting to see St. Peter but
instead I find a small skiing village
at the foot of a mountain,
his white beard shaved for summer.

As music from Heaven spills forth
from Église Saint-Jacques-le-Majeur de La Bolline,
I am convinced that
if there are angels in Heaven
they are certainly musicians,
their only hope to
empty their hearts into
the ears and souls of the masses.

*Wandering*

# Wandering

Dreaming about dreaming is
the surest sign that you're
on a meaningful path to
creating something spectacular.

It's important to realize, at the onset,
that forward is a direction,
no matter how unclear or
misguided it might be.

Forward is the only way and
always leads upstream
to the ultimate point of
originality and clarity.

Be your own guide.

I've spent a lifetime, so far, exploring
the great depths of possibility regarding
everything I have yet to learn and experience and
everyone I have yet to meet.

So each day begins as
a journey to the other side,
to new places where I am not comfortable, for
only through discomfort can I push beyond.

I walk and search and long for
the answers to my questions:

*Where am I going and why, and how will I get there?*

*What am I looking for, and will I know when I find it?*

*Whose face am I longing to see and touch?*

*If I don't look, can I still "see"?*

*If I don't wander, how will I ever uncover all that
I'm missing?*

I'm on a journey with no end,
eyes wide open, and
I feel life's river, its currents,
refreshing but heavy against my legs,
letting me know I'm alive.

The answers will come if I let them.

# A Dog's Life

A bark at the road
grabs my attention and
I watch the animal
in the throes of
a circular frenzy.

A dog chases his tail
for only so long
before realizing he's where
he's supposed to be.

He licks himself
once more as he's done
ten thousand times before and he
sighs and knows he will
see his master again very soon.

# Lines

Sometimes fine and often difficult to see
(maybe we don't wish to see them),
they keep us on the right side
depending on the designer of the line and
which side of the mirror you're standing on.

A sign of the years,
crevices of experience
chiseled in a mask, cured and
hardened by the elements.

A passageway to a destination,
a corridor to the promised land, or
a path to disenchantment.

For some, who are lost and disillusioned,
a powder tonic to numb the mind and soul.

We wait . . .

Rank. Separate. Define. Divide. Cut.

The story of our lives,
a path from conception to death.
If we are lucky and fortunate,
it's squiggly between the two points.

Europeans call it a queue, quite fancy,
but it's still often the blind leading the blind to
the slaughterhouse of wishes and dreams.

I don't want to step in unless I can lead,
for I long to be a pied piper of an enlightened troop.

I can't stand (in) it any more.

# Highlighter

A swipe, often
anxious, reactive, unworthy,
as an acknowledgment of worthiness.

Color me yellow, distinguish me,
not a shade of jaundice but
like a sunflower in the sun.

Give care and thought, if you can,
consider the whole before
selecting the most meaningful.

What are you
but a liquid stick
of determinate power?

Who are you
to hold the stick that gives the
power of lasting acceptance?

Turn the page,
see the other side first,
understand the intent.

Would you rather be a page in a book
where only the border is white, or
a single sentence that stands apart in
a sea of letters?

# Tree of Life

In the beginning,
we saw the coming of the end,
one mistake and then another.
We are not rocks but tree stumps,
and we grow, one small ring a year
as we build a tough outer shell
able to shield us from the elements,
future unending mistakes and influences,
to grow stronger through the ages.
The shell is, however, permeable,
unable to stop the savage blade or
the windswept evil forces of nature, but
even when fallen, apparently dead,
a seed will drop,
the sun will rise, and
with the nurturing rains from above,
we will rise again,
better and stronger than before,
to live and learn and experience
at least one more day,
together, with outstretched arms
reaching for the heavens.

# Slow Burn

Blastoff, by love or spark or flame or unworldly beam, commences the firestorm, a marathon race of a lifetime that we can only hope does not burn out too fast. Neil Young wrote, "It's better to burn out than to fade away," an impactful and scorching statement of the times to be sure, and quoted by Kurt Cobain in his suicide note, but I think Kurt got it wrong and instead I'll wait for the burning and ashes that come by the hand of the gray and lifeless incinerator when I'm finished doing everything I need to do and saying everything I need to say. Why not fly on wings outstretched and lifted by the propulsion of a distant and unknowing but guiding wind. The day is alight, the night a smoldering but still hot ember that brings the new day, enough to kindle the soul for a thousand lifetimes. No matter how smothered, the heart is ablaze like the sun that will live for at least another five billion years, so what's the point in questioning a thing we really know nothing about. Light the wick of a million miles at both ends and lay your bets on which end will hit the centerline first. Then, forget it, because even if you win, the payout is in a denomination you cannot spend. Stop rushing for the finish line that never comes or is washed out, and instead, embrace each step for the weight it carries and mark your own chalk line behind your heel at the end of the new day. You can be a muscle car, burning rubber and leaving your history on the street, which will inevitably be washed away by the raindrops of time, or you can set off on a leisurely ride in your '62 Coupe DeVille, preferably with a loved one in the passenger seat, and see where the road leads you. Take your own, sweet time, if for no other reason than you can.

# Inferno

I was strolling along
when what did I see
but a raging inferno
there in front of me.

I asked the man
about what troubled him so,
and he punched me in the nose
with a roundabout blow.

I said, "Why would you do that
to a stranger on the street?"
He looked down in remorse
as he shuffled his feet.

He hemmed and he hawed
not knowing what or when.
I told him, "Let me have it,"
and he punched me again.

As I picked myself up
and staggered a tad,
I said, "What's wrong with you, man,
have you gone mad?"

The man said, "I'm sorry, you know,
for the wrong I have done.
It just overcomes me
like the weight of a ton.

"It could be this or that,
makes me so mad I can't see,
and I know in the end
it's just the inferno inside of me."

Just then, it came to me quick
with equal parts elation and dread.
I summoned an inferno of my own
and left a fist-print on his forehead.

# Simply Be

**Be seen.**

Be+friend your neighbor.
Be+dazzle every person you meet.
Be+get life.
Be+gin with the action.

**Be heard.**

Be+have better than others.
Be+long to society.
Be+queath your heart.
Be+tray no one.

**Be alive to the fullest.**

Be+tween birth and death, live
Be+yond your wildest dreams.
Be+stir your deepest desires.
Be+lie your years with grace.

**Be outspoken and truthful.**

Be+stow upon yourself the right to fight.
Be+hind the veil of cowardice is not a place.
Be+ware the incompetence of legislators and fools.
Be+hold all the natural wonders of the world.

**Be still and listen.**

Be+lay the love of your friends and family.
Be+lieve in yourself.
Be+come your full potential
Be+fore the end.

**Be.**

# Gene Pool

Fragments of the past and present
intermingled with the dust of the universe
to form something beautiful, new but old,
body and mind and heart from the heavens
reflected in the oceans of fresh, wide eyes
searching the horizon with a prejudiced perception.

The reflection in the mirror not just one
but instead a kaleidoscope of similarities
from all who have come before, blazing,
crying out to the world for recognition,
for history is not only in the past and
the present carries every sparkling star into the future.

We long to embark on a new, uncharted course,
a Magellan of the New Age on a path
in search of a world unspoiled by the hand of man,
a fresh canvas, creating anew, alone, but
we are never alone, never, the palette of history,
vibrant and diverse, guiding the way.

Pure individuality is a futile endeavor,
the best chance a creative recipe manipulation,
a modification of defined and known ingredients,
keeping the flavorful and discarding the foul, and
adding a sprinkle of love to create a new twist
on a favorite dish served to the world.

# A Call from Home

Last year, I received a booming call from a distant number, unknown but familiar, the caller asking for me by name and I sensed a longing in his voice and that I might recognize him. He said his name was Ireland and the calling became clear.

I embarked on a journey to the Emerald Isle to find this man who said we were family and uncover a lineage my ancestors in America only hinted at: great-great grandparents, ghosts, who had traveled across turbulent seas to provide a better life for two sons, the family's first entrepreneurs of the coal trade, each apparently born at the age of sixteen since any record of them before that time was likely destroyed in the Great Chicago Fire of 1871.

When I arrived at Dublin Airport, in line at immigration, flashes of recognition with every glance in any direction, I, no longer lost, saw in the eyes of my compatriots the subtle similarities from genetic traces and lineages that span the centuries that precede me.

It seemed that my brother stamped my passport.

I searched for ancestors with no names, traveled endless roads across the rolling countryside, visited homes with no addresses, and I found that each new face I encountered looked like family, friendly and welcoming and wondering where I've been.

It appears I've been there all along, in spirit but not necessarily body, until now, until this moment in time when I embraced the peoples of the island, and they embraced me, all of us surrounded by glorious waters, love, respect, and the heartfelt music from the plucked strings of their golden harps.

My heart, my lifeline to them is forever open, and I lovingly await a future call, to go home, once again.

# Hijinks Society

Life is one grand practical joke
instigated by unintentional fools.
The practical mind must play along.
It's the only reasonable recourse.
And why not?

Steadfast seriousness,
political correctness, and
unattainable alignment with the "social norm"—
whatever the hell that means—
leads to a dull life and
a heart of stone.

Better to act like a child
with eyes full of endless wonder, and
a fertile mind unencumbered by
needless and senseless boundaries,
who can throw caution to the
gale-force winds of the world.

The youth embrace fun, excitement, adventure.
With old age comes caution,
the first sure sign of the looming visit
from the Grim Reaper, who rides
the cold black train on distant rails but
approaches at an accelerating speed.

Better to advocate a
full agenda of mischief and tomfoolery—
hell, even boisterous and rambunctious escapades—
while one is able since the
ability degrades over time like the
degeneration of an eye.

Once bright and receptive,
vision eventually blurs or is shielded
to the point of blindness,
which, along with caution,
develops inevitably into a constipated soul.

# At the End of the Day

At the end
of the day,
the meaning
of love,

of life,
is merely
the sum of
all the loves

you have plus
the loves you had and
I realize
now

I am
not
quite
complete

in my effort to
define
that
meaning.

Maybe
I'm just
getting
started.

# Hardwired

How fortunate I am that
sometimes a single thought,
first felt as a glowing sensation
at the base of the neck,
triggered into motion through
the programmed firing of neurons,
comes to bear in consciousness and
reality without conscious effort,
but instead as a dictum from
a grand designer of pseudo-genetic code,
from a man unlike most mere mortals,
armed with the digital mastery
necessary to pull a broken young man
from the grasp of the Angel of Death,
from the blood-soaked ditch
littered with smoldering, twisted metal,
to rebuild him in the image of
a different yet equally relevant god.

## No Words Are Necessary

How can I tell you everything that is in my heart?
I cannot find the words.

All I have, all that I am, is in your heart,
cemented into the foundation of our lives together.

I know my feelings are there, within you,
in a heart that beats for both of us.

No words are necessary.

The sparkle in your eyes tells me
everything I need to know.

Even when apart we are together,
never separated, ever.

I am you, and
you are me.

# Notes on Napkins

Writing notes on napkins, in a sense, is such an ancient cliché, but when you're by yourself having a drink in a bar, it beats the alternatives, which are gazing endlessly—like a self-absorbed dope with mind-numbing consequences—into the idiot-slab (iPhone), or making conversation with someone you meet, which you may enjoy, but then again, sometimes it's just better to write than speak. And bar napkins and a pen are always available.

Writing requires thought; speech does not. I can attest to this fact. When forced to speak, I usually have no control over the thoughts I dredge up from the depths of my insanity (we're all basically insane, and it's how we project our insanity verbally that determines if we are normal or not, a determination that is quite subjective and based on the insanity of the person hearing the words), and after a few drinks, all bets are off. Who really knows, or can effectively plan and manage, which words will spring forth and in what order?

If forced to speak, it's important to realize that conversations in a bar have a one-drink limit. Meet someone for a drink, catch up and say all the meaningful words, if there are any, then move on. As I learned from an old customer friend, after the first hour in a bar, the law of diminishing returns kicks in, meaning that with each passing minute, any value, meaningful or memorable in any way, diminishes until you get to the stage of regurgitated, uncensored ramblings, which is a sure, though not obvious, sign that it's time to go home, slip into your casket, and hope that you'll rise from the dead with the sun to see another day and relish the time you have to suffer and harbor the spoken regrets of the prior evening.

Drinking alone, in most cases, eliminates many potential problems, and writing instead of speaking offers the much-needed steps of thought, review, and revision, and revision, and revision . . .

## Why Write Poetry?

Write poetry to . . .

Let the world know that you're alive

Say what is in the heart and mind

Utilize symbolism, metaphor, structure, and form to say what cannot be said any other way

Bleed onto the page the genesis of an idea, a kernel of what may possibly become something more grand

Keep the words flowing, for anyone with an ounce of courage can write a short poem

Test and challenge the conventions of storytelling

Share the perspective of the mind's eye

Get to the point while not spelling out all the details or giving away all the elements of the "secret sauce"

Make a statement, about something, about anything

Let yourself know that you're steadfast in your purpose, kicking and screaming, to release buried passions

Make another person think, a noble goal in an age of misguided and distracted living

Make a difference.

## Pandemic Dilemma 2020

I'm circling the airport at fifteen thousand feet, as I have been for endless months, the only passenger on a plane that I understand will soon run out of fuel.

The first-class section of the aircraft has no seats. In the coach section, all the seats are empty and available, but I am required to sit in the last row, in the middle seat, which is narrow and does not recline.

I need to use the restroom, but the doors are locked. I'm slightly on edge because Captain Arnold, a drunk chimpanzee, is flying the plane, and I understand that he is getting restless and has to pee.

I know this because the flight attendant, Karl, a kind young man with an aggravated rash in his private region, keeps me apprised of the captain's condition.

On the plus side, Karl is an ape whisperer and can translate Captain Arnold's every word, especially his communications with air traffic control.

I understand that we cannot descend until a unanimous nationwide vote approves our flight for landing, which is disconcerting since my life is in the hands of all Americans, who collectively do not have the wherewithal to care.

I have buckled myself tightly into my seat, my hands gripping the armrests, knuckles white.

## 20/20

They say "hindsight is 20/20" but
who are "they" and do they really
know what they're talking about?
I wonder . . .

Often, looking back is a fruitless endeavor,
especially since history is an
unreliable predictor of the future, and
only the here and now is reality.

The eyes may be capable of perfect sight,
but what about the processor of the vision,
the mind, only capable of perception limited
by the mysterious gray matter of the universe?

Not being able to see what
everyone else sees at twenty paces
simply means one must step closer,
a necessary act to grasp the granular details.

In the year of 2020,
what do we see?
What are we searching for?
Do these questions contradict each other?

Clarity and meaning are derived by
busting through life's obscurity,
not with lenses or explanations but
with a trusting and exposed heart.

*Adrift at Sea*

# Adrift at Sea

## I. The Longing

Days, weeks, and months flow through my fingers like water, and I cannot hold on to them, for they puddle at my feet and dissipate into a ghost of nothingness under the hot midday sun, and I harbor a harrowing emptiness. The memories elude me.

I stand at the shoreline, scan the horizon and rippling water, and think and dream about life above and below. When stuck in the sand, I have no bearing, no sense, real or imagined, of the turmoil and serenity of life, for those perceptions also elude me, suppressed by all the fabricated distractions found ashore.

I have seen, heard, and felt all that is natural out on the high seas. The salt air whistles in my ears, stings my eyes, and flavors every perception. Sometimes, when I lie awake in bed late at night and listen to the waves crashing upon the shore, I can recall what I once had and long to meet my mistress, the sea, once again.

## II. The Preparation

I have no choice but to leave the land behind, pull up

the anchor of misguided endeavors that have kept me in a calm but stale harbor for much too long, and venture off again into the unknown I know so well.

There is no need to say goodbye to the few people I hold dear who never knew I was here, but I note in my journal the date she called me away to search for her again. Maybe my history of adventure and self-realization will be of some relevance to a future person, an interested and younger soul, seeking a beacon in troubled waters.

I grab the smallest bag I can find to store my provisions: the Good Book, my journal, a pen and ink, a roll of maps, and the sextant, my grandfather's, a tool with a history that has guided my entire life. Everything else I need is in the stars, sun, and moon, and I will dip into the deep wells of the sea and my heart to guide my journey for the rest of my days.

## III. Leaving Port

At dawn, I board the first ship out, not asking about the destination but comfortable it is going in my direction, and not caring about north or south, just that it is out, away from shore and sailing into the abyss of possibilities.

Agreeing to work for passage was agreeable, for I would gladly pay because the work is necessary if I am ever going to truly appreciate the adventure. I must push my body to the limit in preparation for charting my mind on a similar course. Work is the only way.

We leave the harbor with the seagulls in tow, and I consider who is leading the way. When we are a hundred yards out, my past is already just a figment of memory. I left behind the man I knew onshore and cannot— have no reason to—look back, for I already said goodbye long ago.

I draw in a breath of the fresh, salted air and am rejuvenated, reborn, a child once again, ready to learn and grow and experience the fathomable depths of my soul.

## IV. A Charted Course

The days pass, deliberately, and I experience and feel, physically and mentally, every waking moment. The strong sea wind fills our sails, allowing us to cut through the menacing waters, and the work is brutal, testing my physical abilities and spirit. Time off is time on, for I am unable to sit and watch as my crewmates, who have accepted me—reluctantly at first but then with open arms as they saw my skill and determination—struggle to keep the ship from listing.

At the end of each day, there have been four of them now, our captain steers us to calmer waters. The crew divides and we alternate night shifts, which are the same for me, on or off duty, with sleep the only difference.

Either way, my mind, both conscious and unconscious, is a hurricane. Ideas and story fragments and words whip around in my skull and heart without concern for the possible destructive repercussions.

I write when I can, and when I cannot, the gems of a story at the tip of my nib stay wet until I return, my memory of all that is important remaining fully intact without the bombardment of meaningless drivel and distraction from the land-faring population.

As the pages of my journal lose their blankness, the words restore my purpose. As a crew of one, I am not lonely. I am continually in touch with the people, the characters, who mean something to me, and I learn and grow and become one with them as my stories emerge and develop.

## V. Old Friends

It did not take long to reconnect with my old friends. With true friends, bonding requires no effort at all, happens with the simplest thought, the slightest glance. I am one with the water, wind, sky, stars, sun, and moon. Like our world's first inhabitant, I have no other choice but to accept and embrace the hope of a new existence. An inevitable temptation is always with me to fight and challenge the wind, but I never bite and instead let it guide and transport me to my destination.

My relationship with everything around me is a give-and-take proposition and requires a delicate balance of opposing forces that can easily tip the scales. Often my maps provide an unclear or misguided direction, for the sea is ever changing. All I have are my books, the one I am reading and the one I am writing, to provide a true sense of where I must go, what I must do. The book I am reading provides a perspective of history. The book I am writing dictates the future.

Riding the ebb and flow of the tides and the rising and falling swells of the sea often shakes me, bombards me, with what I need to find my way, and I try not to judge. They are dear friends as well, and while they can sometimes make me sick, through to my core, I realize they are just puppets themselves, their strings manipulated by a much higher force and power, and so I go along for the ride. Any other option is a futile effort to understand the fleeting mysteries of life, which is a gamble, and I am no gambler, and so I carry on to play my own game of chance.

## VI. What Lurks Below

The surface of the sea, whether still or turbulent, acts as an iris of the grandest eye looking into the heavens and it sees, and everything that lurks below sees, and yet as I look down into the glassy cornea I cannot see anything but a dizzying array of blue, black, and green.

The eye of the sea stares at me, torments me, and I wonder what is inside the soul of the beast. The eye winks at me often, sometimes flashing a glint of wonder, and I wish to understand all there is to know but fear that once I'm inside, I will not be able to escape, that I will wish I never made the wish in the first place, and that no matter how hard I try to stay afloat, something will tug on my leg and pull me down into its selfish void.

I consider that the surface of the sea and my skin share a similar purpose. Is all that is inside me so vast and dark? My skin, while thick, is still permeable, but what is on the surface is, like the sea, a blank slate that changes with time, and the permeability flows in only one direction, out, exposing what I want to expose. Do I reveal my wild swings between serenity and turbulence?

I cannot let anyone in. Unlike the sea, I am shallow, but like the sea, I am shadowy and mysterious and fear the unknown, and I take to the sea to explore her, and explore me, and possibly, together, we can figure out what it all means.

## VII. Blown Off Course

On certain days, nothing I do, or the crew does, or the captain directs, makes any sense or difference. I sometimes feel that all attempts at maintaining our charted course are futile. The wind blows too hard from the mouths of the gods. The waves blink furiously in the hurricane of the sea's eye. The sky cries tears of a million restless spirits. Try as we might, she prevails and misdirects our direction.

We have no choice but to join our mistress for the ride into unplanned and uncharted territory. We save our strength for the next battle that will undoubtedly come and settle in to see where the force takes us.

After helping to anchor and secure the ship for the night, I retreat to my quarters and ponder the future. At the moment, I have no sense of my purpose. As the ship and I rock violently with the sea, the most horrific form of a late-night lullaby, I can only hope to keep down, deep within the well of my being, everything I possess and have consumed for sustenance. Letting go will surely be the end of me.

After what feels like a hundred torturous days and nights, the forces relent and the sea calms. I wonder if it is a trick and wait for another sign. All that comes is calm and silence, broken intermittently by the soft creaking of the wood that holds us together and safe.

I hear voices and footsteps on deck and leave the safety of my dungeon with hope for a new day. I stand at the starboard gunwale and gaze in wonder. There is a god, indeed. The turquoise waters still my anxious heart. The sky is so blue and clear that I think again about the only woman I ever loved. The air is so fresh and moist that I fear I can never drink my fill, but I am refreshed and born again to embrace a new day, another chapter of life.

The captain studies the charts, reveals we are off course at least a score of miles, likely more, adding another two days to our journey. I am content. The new place we have come to is mine, for now, and all I have is time.

## VIII. An Angry Sea (The Darkness)

Anger can take many forms, and it is the still and quiet anger that lurks in the depths of a man's soul that scares me. Equally insidious are the repressed animal urges that hide in the shadows beneath the surface of the sea.

Yesterday, after we anchored and secured the sails, a few of the men jumped into the cool, calm water to rinse off the madness of the day. I sat on the deck, my back against the main mast, and noted in my journal the still-fresh images and memories.

The swaying palm trees lining the shore of the ghostly island ahead.

The red-orange glow and warmth of the setting sun.

The brown skin of my comrades, alive and refreshed by the thoughts of another day's end, another destination conquered, one day closer to home, wherever that might be.

Then, I heard the screams of terror that stopped my heart, grasped it like an iron fist. Instinctively, I stood and looked into the water below.

Everything within my vision turned a shade of crimson, a color so evil that stung my eyes and permeated my soul. My ears blocked out all sound and my red vision could not identify the remaining limbs, waving and reaching, hoping for a savior's hand from above. I am thankful that my senses choked, shielding me from the horror of the moment, but the captain made sure to share the details later over harsh whiskey, a tough lesson for the remaining crew members.

As darkness blanketed the sky and sea, I could not make sense of my place and role in the world, for it seems wherever I go, black doom follows.

All I want is to be free.

## IX. A Crew Diminished

On some days, it seems we can make no progress, even when we align perfectly in strength, heart, and mind. With our ranks diminished by three—those we left behind in the brine and who remain only in the deep and dark oceans of our minds, and another in a berth below, legless and blind and waiting to die—we seem adrift. Only our captain maintains a stiff and hardened course, but he is still just a mere mortal.

We are lost.

Death is a recurring torture that remains until the universe collapses and propels us into the next dimension. I wonder what form we will take there. No matter how hard I try to forget the plastic, sleeping faces of the departed, they haunt me, and maybe that is because I am not supposed to forget, ever. As I send off each new casualty into the chasm between our worlds, the ones I have loved the most come back more often and clearer. I wish to dispel the heartache but am glad that the visions remain, because what am I if not my memories?

We remember.

I hunger and thirst for what I cannot take by mouth. With each part of me taken, I look to my brethren for solace and guidance, for a replacement part, but they are dead as well, their passions ebbed and hopes crushed. They need me as I need them. We are helpless and hopeless. Only time can correct our course and align us with the heavens, but our time is as short as the next breath.

We gasp for life.

## X. A New Day

Last night's sleep, while restless and startled by the lightning storm in the sky of my mind, calmed my distressed heart and lifted the anvil from my chest. When all is dire, I take comfort in knowing that Hypnos, the god of sleep, will befriend me once again and settle my soul with a cleansing trance.

The eyes of the sky and crew are clear, floating, white irises splashed with colors from the beginning of time. I see a different world and my comrades share my new wonder. The bread this morning is different, robust and spicy, and I can taste the minerals of the earth where the grain once grew. The wind off the water cools my skin. A sweet scent from the coconut palms ashore lingers in the air. I am refreshed and invigorated.

The memories are fresh in my mind. I think about life and death and what lies in between, and a spark ignites. I must get down onto the page the images and words of the sacred triptych in my mind, opened to expose all the wonder of my past, present, and future. My heart swells with a new meaning I must never forget. I open my journal, dip the golden nib of my pen into the holy black ink, and watch in amazement as my pages fill to overflowing with, what I feel, are the secrets of the universe.

## XI. Onward

I read and relive the handwritten pages of my life, written by an author I am not convinced I genuinely know, and sense a purpose for the first time in years. My words, once merely a chronicle of the times and mere fragments of thought, now tell a story. My story. This journey on the high seas has carried me along a necessary course to instill in me what I always knew was there: the meaning of life.

I can spell the words but cannot speak them yet, for the underlying significance and implications are elusive. By casting myself adrift into unknown and uncharted waters, my blind eyes can see, my deaf ears can hear.

## XII. Uncharted Experience

I had no grand expectations when I took to the sea four full moons ago, wanting only to raise anchor (I can lift it out from the muck and move on, but it forever stays with me, connected as though a fifth limb) and set off into unknown territories with my mind and heart open and willing to accept the inevitable, but the unknown became known in short order and the experiences—unintended and uncharted—seem to mean more than my past or anything I might have planned, and I have learned not too late that planning and expectation are ingredients in a recipe, for a structured existence with boundaries, that nurtures the subtleties of life, those small and individually insignificant but collectively paramount sights, sounds, smells, and flavors of the world that make the meal of life more nourishing and satisfying, and it is these newfound subtleties, unexpected and spectacular, that complement what I perceive through all my senses and make me feel beneath my breastbone a sustaining fullness, and my journey has caused me to view and see the world through different eyes, like those of a soaring eagle, and what I see, no matter how small, appears large in the viewfinder of my mind, with clarity and detail I wish I had had in my preceding years because, in retrospect, I now understand that my sight was often clouded and sometimes blinded, but even my past seems to take on a new meaning now and is flavored differently with the spices of my uncharted experience.

## XIII. Infinite Tailwinds

As my current journey ends, the final port coming into view, I remember what prompted the journey in the first place: my longing and need for her, my mistress, the sea.

Our captain will put the ship into dry dock, and the crew will settle in for a long winter, reconnecting with friends and family and drinking away their hard-earned wages. I will not see nor experience their roller coaster of elation and dread.

My crewmates will not long remember me, for I will fade into the distance like all those who have passed before us, a once-vivid memory soon replaced by a more present thought.

I will remember them.

I cannot stay in port because it was never an option she would allow. She calls for me, endlessly, and knows I will travel the world over in my quest to understand her. She is an unanswerable question from the beginning of civilization.

I will search for her forever.

She pulls me along on a destined course and fills me with the inspiration to take on another day, to confront the challenges that await me, to fulfill my purpose and what I now understand is the sole reason God placed me upon this earth.

She blows gently behind my ear, a flirtatious breath, which sends a tingle up my spine, and then she points me in the noblest of directions and fills my sails to send me on my way.

Another ship awaits me, and it does not matter which one I board; they are all heading to the same ultimate destination, which is my Muse. She is with me but never fully, and it is that fullness I long for.

I open my arms wide, ready to embrace her when we meet again, longing to feel her winds lift and carry me to distant and wondrous places, onward to the experiences that will cure my restless heart and help me formulate the words of my life.

I will search for her until the last breath escapes my lips and the final drop of blood leaks from the nib of my pen.

My journey begins again.

*In the End*

## In the End

There are both lies and truth within these walls,
entombed within deceitful minds of all,
so many spirits lying ever near,
to sow the seeds of fraud and doubt and fear.

I only hope my spark of will ignites,
to set me free into the world so bright,
and leave lightless rooms and lives behind,
to set a course for where the light may shine.

I wonder if I'll find it in the end.

# ACKNOWLEDGMENTS

The author gratefully acknowledges the following individuals who were instrumental in producing this book: manager extraordinaire Lorraine Diaz, the staff at Chicago Arts Press, interior book designer Salvatore Marchetti, illustrator Daniele Serra, and editor Rachel Small.

# ABOUT THE AUTHOR

Dan Burns is the author of seven books, including the novels *A Fine Line* and *Recalled to Life*, and the short story collections *Grace: Stories and a Novella* and *No Turning Back: Stories*. He is also an award-winning writer of stories for the screen and stage. *A Necessary Explosion: Collected Poems* is his first poetry collection, fifteen years in the making. For more information, please visit: www.danburnsauthor.com.

CPSIA information can be obtained
at www.ICGtesting.com
Printed in the USA
LVHW091117150621
690263LV00009B/68/J